Inside Israel's Mossad

The Institute for Intelligence and Special Tasks

Matt Webster

The Rosen Publishing Group, Inc.
New York

Published in 2003 by The Rosen Publishing Group, Inc.
29 East 21st Street, New York, NY 10010

Library of Congress Cataloging-in-Publication Data

Webster, Matt.
Inside Israel's Mossad : the Institute for Intelligence and Special
Tasks/by Matt Webster.
p. cm.—(Inside the world's most famous intelligence agencies)
Summary: Describes the history and current goals of Israel's intelligence service, the Mossad.
Includes bibliographical references and index.
ISBN 0-8239-3815-8 (lib. bdg.)
1. Israel. Mosad le-modi`in ve-tafkidim meyuhadim—Juvenile literature.
2. Intelligence service—Israel—Juvenile literature.
3. Espionage, Israeli—Juvenile literature. [1. Intelligence service—
Israel. 2. Espionage, Israeli.]
I. Title. II. Series.
UB251.I78 W33 2002
327.125694—dc21

2002007398

Manufactured in the United States of America

Cover image: An aerial view of the Knesset, Jerusalem, Israel's house of representatives. The Knesset is named and organized to reflect the Knesset Hagedolah (Great Assembly), the representative Jewish council which met in Jerusalem in the fifth century BC. Information gathered by Mossad is provided to a variety of departments within the Knesset, such as the Immigration and Absorption Committee and the Foreign Affairs and Defense Committee.

INSIDE THE WORLD'S MOST FAMOUS INTELLIGENCE AGENCIES

Contents

Introduction

An ordinary observer would not have noticed anything exceptional about the two men. In fact, they were determined not to attract any attention. The year was 1965, and the pair was sharing a café table in downtown Baghdad. The men chatted in English, but that was not unusual. Many international businessmen and diplomats still passed through Iraq's capital city in those days. One man was older and white haired. The other wore a dark suit typical of business travelers.

The younger man had spent the last two weeks in Iraq working for a British company. He was there selling X-ray equipment to hospitals. Despite his success as a salesman, the job was really just an elaborate cover. It was only a smoke screen designed to turn suspicion away from him. He was traveling under the name George Bacon, but the name and his British passport were fake. Bacon was actually an Israeli spy. He was collecting vital information as an agent of Mossad, Israel's famous intelligence agency. In 1965, Iraq was one of Israel's fiercest enemies. If the wrong person uncovered Bacon's true identity, the Iraqi government would probably execute him. It had happened earlier to unlucky (or unprepared) spies in his position.

The older man gave only the name Joseph. He was the key to one of the most complicated operations that Mossad had ever attempted. He was a Jew, part of a tiny minority in

In 1966, a pilot escaped from Iraq to Israel with a MiG-21. This Russian-built fighter plane was much more powerful than Israel's fighter plane, the Mirage. Studying the performance of the MiG-21 enabled the Israeli air force to determine its weaknesses and prevail over its enemies in the Six-Day War.

Iraq. Months before, he had contacted Mossad agents working in Europe. He made them an astounding proposal. Joseph told Mossad that he knew an Iraqi air force pilot. His pilot friend was willing to bring Israel a treasure that Mossad wanted very much. With Mossad's help, the pilot would fly to Israel in a Soviet MiG-21 aircraft.

For the Israelis, obtaining the top-secret, high-tech airplane would deal a devastating blow to their enemies worldwide. Many of these adversaries relied on weapons and military equipment made by the Soviet Union. Stealing the MiG-21, however, would not be as easy as jumping in the cockpit and turning on the ignition. The operation would require a highly organized international spy network and perhaps millions of dollars. Everyone involved, including the pilot's family, would be in grave danger if the plan failed. Success was not guaranteed. But Mossad felt the risks would be worth the rewards.

Chapter One

New Nation, New Problems

When Israel announced its establishment in 1948, it sat on a small triangle of land that had previously been a British colony called Palestine. The new nation was surrounded by enemies who were determined to destroy it. Arab residents of the former Palestine did not accept the declaration of a Jewish state. They considered the area to be their own homeland. In addition, the founding of Israel enraged the neighboring Arab nations of Syria, Egypt, Jordan, and Lebanon. The leadership of these countries saw Israel as a reminder of the colonial period, when foreign Western powers controlled the region. These countries deployed their armies to destroy Israel from all sides. At the time, most people around the world did not think Israel's outnumbered military forces could possibly win the war.

The War of Independence turned out to be one of the greatest upsets in modern history. Despite its inferior numbers, the Israeli army managed to defend its borders. As the Bible describes, the Jews' ancestors sacrificed everything in their long struggle to build a nation under Mount Zion. Now Jews had again fought bravely, and finally regained control of their ancient homeland. Because of their intense dedication to the re-establishment of this Jewish state, they often referred to themselves as Zionists. After 1948, the term

Israeli intelligence played a large part in Israel's ability to survive Arab attacks in its 1948 War for Independence. In the years before the war, Israeli Wolfgang Lotz had been infiltrating the Egyptian military and political institutions to gather valuable intelligence information. Many other spies for Israel had been ferreting out vital secrets throughout the Arab countries.

"Zionist" would refer to anyone who defended Israel's security and believed in her right to exist.

The Jews never could have won the War of Independence without collecting military intelligence. Although "intelligence" just means information, it suggests the kind of knowledge that somebody else would prefer to keep secret. For example, imagine that you know a person named Bob. Bob is cheating on his girlfriend and you know about it. This knowledge is a piece of intelligence about Bob that could be very important to his girlfriend. It could be important to Bob, too, depending on how you use it.

For years before the 1948 war, spies working for Jewish groups had been secretly collecting information in foreign countries. Some of them managed to obtain attack plans from the armies of Egypt and Jordan. This stolen intelligence helped Israel to plan its own military strategies. The result was the successful establishment of the Jewish state.

David Ben-Gurion was the first prime minister of Israel. He had been a Zionist leader for many years before 1948. Ben-Gurion always realized that intelligence was crucial to Israel's security. In 1951, he ordered the establishment of Mossad, a secret agency to collect intelligence in foreign lands.

This is how Ben-Gurion described the main goal of Israeli intelligence at the F.A.S. Intelligence Research Program's Web site:

> *Since its creation [our state] has been under siege by its enemies. Intelligence constitutes the first line of defense . . . we must learn well how to recognize what is going on around us.*

David Ben-Gurion, Israel's first prime minister, is shown here in 1965 walking with Israeli citizens. Behind him flies the flag of Israel.

An Uncertain Future

When the War of Independence ended in January 1949, Israel's problems were far from over. The casualties of the conflict were heavy on both sides. Four thousand Jewish soldiers and two thousand civilians were killed. The Arab armies and civilian populations suffered even heavier casualties. Although Israel rejoiced in its victory and the chance to strengthen its new nation, everyone knew that peace would not last forever. Egypt and the other surrounding countries still had powerful armies, and they were extremely bitter over their defeat by the Israelis.

There was another result of the 1948 war that remains an important issue in Israeli politics today. During the conflict, 750,000 Palestinian Arabs fled to neighboring countries, or were forced to leave by the Israeli army. Jewish settlers went to live in the communities the Palestinians left behind. Most of the war refugees went to Jordan, to the east, and Lebanon, to the north. For many years they were not accepted as citizens in any country. For Palestinian Arabs, the 1948 war was devastating. Within a few years, the Jewish population of Israel doubled, completely changing the face of the land Palestinians considered home. Despite their defeat, the Palestinians held on to the belief that they would one day return home and establish their own state. The Palestinian question is still the most complicated and troubling problem that faces Israel today.

Israel is a relatively small place whose very existence is unpopular with many other countries around the world. It has always been in a unique political situation. Although there have been periods of peace in Israel since 1948, there have also been many wars. Israel must constantly be on guard. The next painful conflict could be right around the corner. More so than many other countries, Israel always has to be prepared for the worst. This is the reason that Israel's intelligence agencies have to be extremely effective. Because Israel's future is so connected with international politics and intelligence gathering, even sworn enemies say Mossad is the most powerful of all of these agencies.

Mossad Departments and Goals

The word "Mossad" means "an institute" in Hebrew, the leading official language of Israel. The full name in English

On Thursday March 28,1996, Shin Bet Chief Carmi Gilon, center, talks to reporters in Jerusalem after a commission of inquiry into the assassination of Yitzhak Rabin found Gilon directly responsible for allowing it to happen. Gilon resigned as a result, and the commission said it agreed with Gilon's decision.

is the Institute for Intelligence and Special Tasks. When new agents, or officers, enter the agency, they learn never to use the word "Mossad." Instead they refer to the agency as "the office." Mossad is one of the most secretive organizations in the world.

Israel has other intelligence agencies in addition to Mossad. An agency called Shin Bet, the acronym in Hebrew for security service, is responsible for the security of Israel's citizens inside the country's borders and in the occupied territories. Another agency, called Amman, the acronym in Hebrew for the army's security branch, analyzes military intelligence.

Although the focus of the organization has changed over the years, Mossad is now specifically responsible for collecting information in foreign countries and for communicating with foreign intelligence agencies that are friendly with Israel. In order to collect intelligence effectively, Mossad carefully separates work into distinct areas of knowledge, or compartments, which are as specific as possible. In this way, each worker can concentrate on his or her special duty. The division of duties also helps prevent information from being leaked to people who do not need to know it. This principle is called compartmentalization.

Compartmentalization does not only exist in intelligence work. It is also an important part of managing any industry or a large corporation. In many ways, Mossad operates as if it were a business. Many long-time Mossad agents have moved on to successful careers in private industry after leaving the agency. While the focus in the corporate world is to make as much money as possible, the ultimate goal of Mossad is to collect intelligence that can be useful to Israel and its allies. After collecting the right intelligence, Mossad is responsible for using the information to conduct secret activities that will protect or benefit Israel.

It's interesting to note that the majority of intelligence Mossad gathers comes from sources that are available to everybody. They include newspapers, television, and the Internet. Although these are the largest categories of information, they are not the most important. Other intelligence comes from surveillance, which means hidden observation of people or organizations without their knowledge.

Who's Who

Secrecy and security are important in this type of work. If information about Mossad operations ever reaches the public,

Danny Yatom was forced to resign as director of Mossad after an operational failure in 1997.

it happens a long time after an operation has taken place. As a result of this policy, some details of Mossad's operations have only recently become public.

Until 1996, the identity of the director of Mossad was kept secret. Danny Yatom became director that year. When a newspaper publicly revealed his name, many Israeli officials were enraged by the breach of security. Mossad has since become slightly more open. Former officers, or people who worked for intelligence agencies in other countries, have gradually revealed information. The current director is Ephraim Halevy, who has worked at many different jobs in the agency. He is also the oldest man to serve as Mossad's director.

Although the organization of Mossad is very complicated, it is estimated that it employs from 1,200 to 2,000 people at any time. It has at least six departments.

All Mossad officers go through an intensive training program before entering the office. Trainers test officers' ability to keep secrets and to think fast in difficult situations. Each officer receives a Beretta handgun and learns how to use it.

The Collections Department

The largest department in the agency, the Collections Department, runs intelligence bureaus in foreign countries. The offices always have a cover, or a false identity. They do not say "Mossad" on the door. Often the agency disguises its activities as a diplomatic organization, or as a business that is not related to intelligence. In fact, Mossad often sets up real businesses in foreign countries

In December 2000, Ephraim Halevy gave the first public speech made by a Mossad director. This soft-spoken man appeared to favor the idea of land-for-peace negotiations with the Palestinians.

to provide cover for some of its intelligence operations. Most of the employees at these companies have no idea that the business is a front for Mossad. If the company is successful and makes a profit, Mossad can use the money to finance other espionage activities.

The Political Action and Liaison Department

The Political Action and Liaison Department is responsible for communicating with intelligence agencies in countries that have good relationships with Israel. "Liaison" means connecting, or communicating.

The United States is an example of a country that works closely with Israel. The United States's foreign intelligence agency is called the Central Intelligence Agency (CIA). Mossad provides the CIA with intelligence of great value to the United States. In exchange, the CIA provides important intelligence to Mossad. The agencies do not share everything, however, and there have been some major conflicts between them over the years. The most damaging episode was the 1986 "Pollard Affair," in which an Israeli spy was caught operating in the U.S. Navy. Even friendly spy networks have some information that they wish to keep secret.

Special Operations Division

The third department, the Special Operations Division, is probably the most secretive part of Mossad. The Special Operations Division conducts activities including assassinations and operations involving foreign military groups. In addition, the Special Operations Division takes care of activities that may be dangerous or unpopular with local authorities in the country in which they are operating.

Lohamah Psichlogit Department

The fourth major division in Mossad is the Lohamah Psichlogit Department (LAP). LAP (Literature and Publications) is responsible for propaganda, which means giving out information that will influence people's opinions or help Israel in some way. Of course, propaganda is not always the truth. As a matter of fact, the official slogan of Mossad is this quotation from the Bible: "By way of deception, thou shalt do war."

This senior intelligence officer in Israel points to Yasser Arafat's alleged signature on documents during a press conference in 2002. She is supporting the claim made by Israeli intelligence that the Palestinian leader helped finance terrorist attacks in Israel.

The Research Department

The Research Department gathers detailed intelligence reports from all over the world. It supplies this information to any agent who may need it.

Technology Department

The final main division of Mossad is the Technology Department. The Technology Department develops cutting-edge electronics and computer systems to help Mossad gain intelligence that can help protect Israel.

Sayanim

In addition to its professional staff, Mossad has working relationships with many other people who can be helpful in

These Israeli soldiers were photographed in Jerusalem on June 8, 1967. They are standing outside the United Nations headquarters, which Israel captured from Jordan during the Six-Day War.

specific situations. Mossad knows people around the world who are not professional spies, but who are Jewish and will gladly help Israel. Mossad knows it can call on them if an agent is conducting a local operation. These Jews, called sayanim, often have a professional specialty or position that can be useful to undercover agents. For example, if a sayan owns a car rental agency in London, he can lend cars to Mossad agents without asking a lot of questions. He may even provide the service free of charge. Often sayanim are people with good business or political connections.

Types of Intelligence

The best kind of information a Mossad agent can receive is called human intelligence, or humint. This describes information that comes from a human source, someone who gives information directly to a spy. In many cases, the source does not know that he or she is giving information to an intelligence agent. Although humint is only a very small percentage of the information Mossad collects, it is definitely the most important.

Another kind of intelligence is signal intelligence, or sigint. Sigint is intelligence that is received over radio waves. Using sophisticated equipment, it is possible to conduct two-way communications, for a short time, at very specific radio frequencies. This is a relatively safe way to exchange information secretly.

In addition to conducting secret communications, Mossad also seeks to find and decode messages that may come from Israel's enemies. One example of important sigint came during the Six-Day War of 1967, when Israel discovered a secret radio communication between its enemies, King Hussein of Jordan and Abdel Nasser of Egypt in which Nasser urged Hussein to join the battle against Israel while hiding Egypt's military defeat.

Today Israel is a leader in the field of high-tech electronics. Mossad puts tremendous effort into developing computer systems that can find and maintain large amounts of information. It has developed a computer system called PROMIS, which is a large and very powerful intelligence database. The agency also sells its PROMIS technology to other nations.

Chapter Two

Beginnings of Mossad

When Israel's first prime minister, David Ben-Gurion, announced the foundation of Mossad in 1951, he made it very clear that the prime minister would have ultimate control over the agency's activities. He named Reuven Shiloah as the first director. "...Shiloah will work under me, will operate according to my instruction, and will report to me constantly about his work," said Ben-Gurion in *Israel's Secret Wars,* by Ian Black and Benny Morris. The relationship between Mossad's leadership and Israel's prime minister has remained very close to this day.

Espionage is difficult work, and Mossad did not achieve success immediately. At first, there was a great deal of disagreement within Israel's intelligence community about how to do things. Military intelligence officers wanted control over certain areas of operation that had been given to Mossad. As a result, many people lost their jobs and there was a lot of confusion. In addition, two major scandals took place shortly after the agency's birth. All of this assured that Reuven Shiloah would not serve as the director for very long.

Throughout their history, Zionists have strongly encouraged Jews all over the globe to return to their ancient homeland as immigrants. For years before the foundation of Israel, when Great Britain controlled the region, this was difficult and sometimes illegal. But Jewish settlers continued secretly to bring in new immigrants to Israel. They correctly believed that a larger Jewish population would help build a strong Jewish state. Jews often refer to this return to the homeland with the Hebrew term *aliyah,* meaning "to ascend." At the time of Israel's establishment in 1948, the Jewish population of the country was about 650,000.

In the first half of the twentieth century, anti-Semitism around the world made this immigration even more urgent. Anti-Semitism refers to prejudice, or hatred, against Jewish people. Throughout their long history, Jews have constantly been the victims of some form of anti-Semitism. From the late 1930s to the end of World War II in 1945, Adolf Hitler's Nazis tried systematically to kill all of Europe's Jews in the brutal campaign known as the Holocaust. During this period, Holocaust survivors streamed into Palestine and then Israel. Unfortunately, most European Jews never made it to their biblical homeland. Six million Jews ultimately died as victims of Hitler's Nazi death camps. The terror of the Holocaust made Zionists even more determined to finally create a haven where Jews could live in safety.

After Israel's establishment in 1948, many Arab states were determined to sabotage Israel's statehood. Many of these countries had small groups of Jews living in their territories as a poor, oppressed minority, whom they would not allow to relocate to Israel. As a result, Israeli intelligence services took responsibility for making contact with these Jews to help them emigrate in secret.

During the 1945 liberation of the Nordhausen concentration camp in Germany, Allied troops walk among the corpses of slave laborers who had been starved to death by their Nazi captors.

This photo from 1969 shows two of fourteen Iraqis who were executed in Baghdad for being spies for Israel. Nine of the hanged men were Jews. Many world leaders, including U.N. secretary U Thant denounced this event. Israeli premier Levi Eshkol observed that the only crime committed by the nine men was that they were Jewish.

Building Spy Networks and Watching Them Fall

In Iraq, Israel spent years carefully building a spy network. The goal was to bring Iraqi Jews to Israel. Just nine weeks after the foundation of Mossad, however, Iraqi authorities uncovered this network. They arrested two Israeli spies, as well as dozens of Iraqi Jews. Israel had also bribed many Arabs for help with the operation. The Iraqi police threw most of these people in jail and severely tortured the Israeli spies. Iraq finally released them after receiving a large sum of money from Israel in exchange for their return.

Mossad's second big scandal was less than a year later. A spy named Theodore Gross had been collecting intelligence for Israel in Rome for years. Mossad considered him to be an important agent. Around the beginning of 1952, a Shin Bet officer named Isser Harel received evidence that Gross was actually a double agent. He was receiving payments from Egypt, one of Israel's enemies. Without revealing that he knew what was happening, Harel traveled to Rome to meet Gross. Harel convinced the double agent to return to Israel. Upon his return, Gross was convicted of treason and went to jail, where he died years later.

These unpleasant beginnings took their toll on Reuven Shiloah. Because of the difficulties, Ben-Gurion fired him in September 1952. He had been the director for only fifteen months.

Chapter Three

Little Isser Makes His Mark

Isser Harel, who had helped expose some of the failures of Mossad in its early days, became the agency's second director. Harel also worked for many years in the service of pre-state Jewish intelligence networks.

Isser Harel was only about four feet, eight inches tall. As a nickname, many people called him Little Isser, as there was a "Bigger Isser," Isser Beeri, a high-ranking intelligence officer. Little Isser had come to Palestine from the small eastern European country of Latvia in 1930. In his younger days he worked on a kibbutz, or Jewish community farm. The kibbutz movement was a big part of Israel's early economy. This experience influenced Harel's views of Israeli society. When trying to find intelligence agents, he looked for people with a kibbutz background, or kibbutzim, because he felt they had a good understanding of Arabs. On the other hand, it often seemed that Harel did not have a high opinion of Orthodox, or strictly religious, Jews.

When Harel came to Mossad in 1952, the agency had just experienced some serious losses. Under his patient leadership, "the office" began to find its direction.

Isser Harel, the second chief of Israel's Mossad, wrote *The House on Garibaldi Street*, the true story of Mossad's audacious kidnapping of Nazi Adolf Eichmann from Argentina. Harel's book, published in 1975, won worldwide acclaim and was translated into more than twenty languages.

Aliyah

The idea of Jews returning to Israel is defined in Hebrew by the word "aliyah." One of Mossad's most important projects of this period was bringing Jews to Israel from the North African country of Morocco. In 1954, Morocco was still a colony of France, but this would change on March 2, 1956. France had agreed that Morocco's royal family would officially take control of the country on that day. In November 1954, Mossad sent an agent named Shlomo Havilio to Morocco to check on the condition of its Jewish population.

In the late 1950s, North Africa was coming to the end of a long period of European control. After his visit, Havilio reported back to Mossad that he feared Morocco's Jews would be in danger when the country became independent from France. He said that Israel should create an organization to help Moroccan Jews defend themselves and even immigrate to Israel. David Ben-Gurion and Mossad also realized that they had to put the operation in place before Morocco became independent. They hoped that the French government would assist them.

This photo shows a typical Jewish ghetto in Marrakesh, Morocco, in 1955. As early as the eleventh century, Jews were forced by Moroccan Muslims to live in filthy, impoverished ghettos called *mellahs*, named after the Arabic word for salt. Moroccan Jews were often forced to salt the heads of executed prisoners before they were put on public display.

In 1954, Mossad agents in Paris met with French officials to discuss the issue. They agreed that Israel could bring 700 Moroccan Jews to Israel each month, without telling the authorities in Morocco. Mossad decided to use its office in Paris as a base for the operation. Undercover agents used secret radio transmitters and receivers to communicate between France and Morocco.

Eventually they assembled a network of nearly 600 Moroccan Jews to help them. Many were sent to Israel or France to receive military training, in order to defend fellow Jews if necessary. Mossad agents inside Morocco also organized transportation routes across the Mediterranean Sea to Israel. Usually, the immigrants were brought first to the

British territory of Gibraltar, near Spain. There they would change boats and continue on to the end of their journey.

Eventually the Moroccan police caught on to what was happening. In 1956, a short time after Morocco achieved independence from France, Morocco's leadership closed down some camps where Jews waiting to leave the country were stationed. They also made Jewish immigration to Israel officially illegal.

Mossad expected this would happen. Although their task became much more dangerous, agents continued to use the secret underground immigration network. They established contacts with Moroccan officials and police to keep them well informed. They also handed out bribes whenever necessary to keep the operation going. Years later, Isser Harel revealed that these bribes added up to around half a million dollars.

At the end of 1960, a ship named the *Pisces* crashed into rocks near Gibraltar. Forty-two Moroccan Jews, a Mossad radio operator, and one crewman drowned. After the sinking of the *Pisces*, Mossad publicly insisted that Moroccan Jews had the right to emigrate if they so chose. Morocco's secret police reacted harshly. They arrested around twenty Jews who had helped the operation and tortured them.

Israel continued publicly to denounce the policies of the Moroccan government. U.S. president John F. Kennedy and French president Charles de Gaulle expressed their support for the Jewish immigration to Israel. Shortly after, Muhammed V, the king of Morocco, died and his son, Hassan II, came to power. Hassan II quickly changed the emigration policy and issued group passports to all Jews who wanted to leave. Within two years, almost the entire Jewish population of Morocco had gone to Israel. Bringing in many thousands of new citizens to Israel was the most successful immigration operation ever conducted by Mossad.

Kidnapping a Nazi

Mossad director Isser Harel took on another project in the late 1950s that would show the world the effectiveness of Israel's intelligence services. In late 1957, Harel got an intriguing

This is an undated photograph of Nazi Adolf Eichmann. After World War II, Eichmann escaped to Argentina where he was tracked and brought to Israel by Mossad to stand trial. While he claimed that he did not have an important role in the murder of millions of Jews, many witnesses identified him as having been fifth in command of the Nazis.

tip from a half-Jewish German judge. The judge claimed to have information about a former Nazi named Adolf Eichmann.

For Holocaust survivors around the world, Eichmann was a symbol of Nazi brutality. From his position at the Nazi Office for Jewish Emigration, Eichmann directed the massive operation that sent millions of Jews to concentration camps and, eventually, to their deaths. After the war, Eichmann disappeared. No one knew whether he was dead or alive.

In his childhood, Isser Harel had witnessed the Nazi's cruelty firsthand. The job of finding Eichmann and bringing him to justice was a crucial mission for him.

The original source said that Eichmann was living with his family in the city of Buenos Aires, Argentina. He was using a false name to conceal his identity. The source even gave an address where he believed Eichmann was living. Harel cautiously sent agents to Germany and Argentina to check out the story. The information was wrong.

Gathering intelligence is usually a very slow process. After almost two years of waiting on the Eichmann case, Isser Harel received information from a different source who also said Eichmann was in Buenos Aires. By comparing the stories of his two sources, Harel decided there was a good chance that Mossad could find the man responsible for the deaths of millions of people.

He sent experienced undercover agents to Argentina. After a good deal of investigation, they found the man they believed was Eichmann. Using the name Ricardo Klement, he was living with his family in a small house in the suburbs. With cameras hidden inside of briefcases, the agents took pictures of Klement. They also photographed the house, the street, and the surrounding area.

By analyzing these photographs, Harel was able to prove that Ricardo Klement was almost definitely Adolf Eichmann. He decided that Eichmann could be captured in Argentina, then secretly brought to Israel to stand trial for his crimes against humanity. Of course, the Argentinean government would have prevented this mission had they known in advance about the plan. The job had to be done in complete secrecy.

Adolf Eichmann stands in a bulletproof cage in 1962 during his trial for crimes against the Jewish people, crimes against humanity, and war crimes. After more than 100 witnesses testified against him, Eichmann defended himself by saying he was just obeying orders. A fellow Nazi reportedly said about Eichmann: "He would leap laughing into the grave because the feeling that he had five million people on his conscience would be for him a source of extraordinary satisfaction."

Harel put together a team of experienced undercover agents. Each had a special role. One man was an expert in forgery. His job was to create false documents for all of the people involved, because they would all be traveling under assumed names. Some agents were responsible for following Ricardo Klement, or Eichmann, without his knowing it. Other men would capture this man and bring him back to Israel. A doctor was sent to make sure the prisoner was safe and in good health. The leader of the team was Rafi Eitan, a veteran of Israel's intelligence services.

The team arrived in Buenos Aires in May 1960, with the goal of kidnapping Eichmann. They rented safe houses around the city, places where they could sleep and meet without attracting attention. Posing as tourists, they followed him from a distance and observed his daily routine. Finally, after weeks of preparation, they waited for Eichmann as he walked from a bus stop to his house. Driving up behind him, Rafi Eitan and another agent jumped out of the car and dragged in Eichmann. They took him to one of the safe houses and interrogated him.

It did not take long for the former Nazi officer to admit his real identity. The team then arranged to put him on a special flight bound for Israel. They forced Eichmann to put on an Israeli mechanic's uniform, then fed him a lot of whisky. When the Argentinean security guards saw the Israeli mechanics helping their sleeping, drunken friend onto the plane, they laughed and didn't ask for identification. The team got Eichmann onto the plane and took him to Israel.

Eichmann was tried for crimes against humanity and was eventually hanged for his role in the Holocaust. The case made a strong statement about Israel's ability to gather information around the world. It also showed that Israel was not afraid to take action, when necessary, against its enemies.

Chapter Four

Politics and Propaganda

Throughout the 1950s, Israel continued to assert itself politically, which was quite a challenge. Although military clashes ended in 1948, Israel still had a very uneasy relationship with its neighbors. The situation around its borders remained unstable. In 1952, Egypt was taken over by a group of military officers. General Gamal Abdel Nasser emerged as Egypt's leader.

In 1954, Israeli intelligence services suffered a major setback. A network of Israeli spies had been operating within Egypt. Their goal was to conduct sabotage and propaganda operations inside enemy territory. The network was called Unit 131. Israeli military intelligence and Mossad shared responsibility for the unit. Mossad director Isser Harel was not happy with this arrangement. He thought that Mossad should be in charge of all foreign operations. Harel also thought Unit 131 was disorganized and that the agents involved were unprepared. He was right, but Israel learned too late.

In July 1954, Unit 131 began a bombing campaign in cities around Egypt. No one was hurt and the goal was not severe destruction. Instead, the Israeli spies wanted the bombing to have a psychological effect. The idea was to make other countries, including Great Britain and the United

In this 1955 photograph, Israeli signal corps trucks are on maneuvers in Tel Aviv. According to an Israeli army communiqué at the time, defense forces had recently attacked Egyptian "suicide commando" bases near the Suez Canal.

States, falsely believe that Egypt was a hostile country. This would give Israel stronger allies in its conflict against Egypt.

A Unit 131 agent was attempting to plant a bomb in a cinema when it went off in his pocket. The Egyptian police caught him. He was tortured during his interrogation and his revelations led to the arrest of the entire Unit 131 network. For Egypt, the operation was proof that Israel was conducting a secret war inside its territory. This incident helped to justify Egypt's continued hostilities against Israel. For Israel's military and intelligence establishment, it was a disaster.

Egypt executed several of the spies. In 1955, after a long series of cross-border raids by Palestinians, supported by Egypt, the Israeli military responded by bombing an Egyptian airbase in Gaza, near the border. This escalated existing tensions.

The Suez Crisis

In July 1956, Egypt took control of the Suez Canal. Under the pretext of opening the canal for all vessels, France and Britain attacked Egypt in October. In November, Egypt closed off the canal by sinking forty ships.

The Suez Canal, which connects the Mediterranean Sea and the Red Sea, runs through Egypt. It is necessary for direct passage of ships from western Europe to the Middle East and Asia. It is particularly important for international commerce. For example, countries that export a lot of oil from the Middle East rely on the Suez as a trade route. Israel also relied on safe passage through the canal to import and export goods from Asia. After the 1948 war, the Egyptian navy would not let Israeli ships pass through the canal.

When the British army left its bases in 1955, the colonial era ended for Egypt. The same year, General Abdel Nasser announced that Egypt would conduct a large arms buildup. Nasser bought the weapons from the Soviet bloc through Czechoslovakia.

In 1955 the British navy also left the Suez Canal. Until this time, the canal had been under international control. In July 1956, Nasser declared that the Suez Canal was now the property of Egypt alone. Many countries were affected by the seizure of the Suez Canal.

This photo was shot during the Suez Canal crisis in November 1956. British and French troops are visible through this bullet-pierced window as they unload equipment in Port Said. The crisis marked major shifts in the powers of western Europe. Britain's colonial and imperial power was rapidly decreasing as Cold War politics gathered momentum.

Israeli intelligence services played a large part in the 1956 Suez conflict. After Nasser seized control of the canal, Israeli agents met with representatives of the CIA and French intelligence services. For all of these countries, it was important for the canal to stay under international control. France, Great Britain, and Israel agreed to retake the Suez using military force. They made an agreement to have Israel invade the Sinai Peninsula. The Sinai, which is Egyptian territory, is a great desert stretching between the Israeli border and the Suez Canal. After Israel invaded the Sinai, the air forces of Great Britain and France would bomb Egyptian bases near the canal.

Before Israel moved into the Sinai Peninsula, covert agents spread false information that Israel was about to invade

Jordan, not Egypt. Mossad also fed bad information to people inside Egypt. The channel, or the person passing the intelligence to the Egyptians, was not aware that he was spreading Israeli propaganda. He may have been an enemy spy who thought the information would actually help Egypt.

The propaganda campaign worked. The Sinai invasion completely surprised the Egyptian army. Israeli tanks moved in and took control of the Sinai Desert without much resistance from Egypt.

The Egyptian navy withdrew, and the canal remained under international control. Israel had worked together with Western powers to maintain some regional stability, although American and Soviet interventions forced the Israeli, British, and French troops to leave their positions shortly afterward.

The operation also succeeded partly because Israel and its allies were able to keep the Sinai invasion a secret. Good intelligence does not only involve trying to find out other people's secrets. It is equally important to protect your own secrets. Using the same strategy, Israel would have another major victory in the Six-Day War of 1967.

Another interesting fact of the Suez crisis was that Mossad exchanged information with the United States's foreign intelligence agency, the CIA. James Angleton, the director of the CIA, had been in close contact with Israel for years. The CIA wanted the Suez Canal to remain under international control. The two agencies found they could help each other.

Mossad scored big points with the CIA by sharing some secrets about the Soviet Union, which had been the United

States's enemy during the Cold War. In the 1950s, Mossad found out that the new Soviet leader, Nikita Khrushchev, in famous speech, denounced the former Soviet leader, Joseph Stalin, as a criminal. Israel had a good network of spies within Russia, where there was a highly placed Jewish population. The speech helped the CIA understand the current thinking inside the Soviet leadership, which was very closed and secretive at that time.

Operation Damocles and the End of Little Isser

Like politics, intelligence is extremely competitive and sometimes bitter work. In fact, intelligence and politics are quite closely related. Sometimes intelligence agents get into disagreements with other agents from the same side. This can create a political, or tense, attitude between people who are supposed to be working together. The same thing frequently happens in the corporate world.

This is what happened to Little Isser Harel. After ten years as Mossad director, he had seen a lot of major covert missions succeed and some fail. By 1962, people within Israel were starting to question Mossad's policies. Harel was considered to be obsessed with control. All great spymasters have this aspect to their personality to some extent. When people in Israel's military intelligence and the press started to criticize Mossad, and Harel specifically, he did not back down in the power struggle. He put up a strong fight, but he lost his job. Harel remained bitter enemies with the people who forced him out of Mossad until his death.

In July 1962, Abdel Nasser publicly displayed a new rocket that his country would use in its fight against Israel. This high-tech missile had a much longer range than the weapons Egypt had used before, giving Egypt the ability to attack any target inside Israel. This development was alarming.

Israel's military intelligence agency was furious with Isser Harel. The chief of military intelligence at the time was a general named Meir Amit. Amit felt that Harel had not been

Gamal Abdel Nasser was president of Egypt from 1956 to 1970. He assumed power in 1952 after a coup overthrew British control and Egypt's king. He was officially elected president in 1956. He was considered a hero in the Arab world because he modernized Egypt.

concentrating enough on the security of Israel and its citizens, but on operations with political impact. Instead, Harel had focused on the hunt for Eichmann, who no longer posed a threat to Jews. In another famous case, Harel had conducted a painstaking search for a young boy named Yossele Schumacher who had been kidnapped from his parents by his grandfather, who wanted to raise him as an Orthodox Jew. Eventually Mossad found the boy, but some of Harel's colleagues felt they were spending too much time on these kinds of projects. They argued that Israel's neighbors were busy plotting its destruction. Meir Amit felt that Mossad had not done enough to warn

Israel about the weapons programs that were taking place in Egypt.

Harel tried to address the problem, but eventually it led to his resignation from Mossad. Shortly after Nasser displayed the new rocket, Harel shared a new piece of intelligence with Israel's prime minister, David Ben-Gurion. Harel had learned that the rockets were being developed for Egypt by a group of German scientists. With Ben-Gurion's approval, Harel put together a campaign to harass and intimidate some of these scientists. It was called Operation Damocles. In February 1963, Mossad attempted to assassinate one of the scientists, who had also worked for the Nazis in World War II. Isser Harel was so involved in the operation that he personally waited all night with the hit man. He wanted to make sure the assassination went perfectly, but it didn't. The Mossad hit man missed the target, and the bullet went into the man's car instead.

In March 1963, Operation Damocles became a public embarrassment for Israel when two Mossad agents were arrested in Switzerland. They had been threatening the daughter of one of the German scientists and were also attempting to blackmail him.

The bad publicity was finally too much for Harel, who resigned on March 25, 1963. He still insisted that he was not to blame for the problems of Mossad, but he had to quit. His mentor, Ben-Gurion followed shortly.

The next director of Mossad was Meir Amit, Harel's archenemy. A few hours after Harel's resignation, Amit walked into Mossad's headquarters in Tel Aviv and took over the position.

Chapter Five

A New Chief Takes Charge

Meir Amit is a legendary figure in Israel's history. Born in Palestine, Amit worked his way up through the ranks of Israel's military. Eventually he reached the second highest office in the army. After a parachuting accident, he had to give up his position as a general. Moshe Dayan, Israel's minister of defense, then asked Amit to become the new chief of military intelligence. Although he had no intelligence experience, Amit was very serious about his work. During his time as Mossad's chief, Amit established many of the methods that have made Mossad one of the most accomplished and revered intelligence agencies in the world.

MiG-21

Shortly after Amit joined Mossad, he received a very interesting offer. A man walked into Israel's embassy in Paris. He said his name was Salman and he could arrange to give Israel a top-secret jet fighter, the Soviet MiG-21. His fee for the job was $1 million.

The technical specifications of this airplane were extremely important to Israel's military. Many of Israel's

After fourteen men, including nine Jews, were hanged in Iraq in 1969 for being Israeli spies, Jews demonstrated peacefully outside the Iraq Embassy in Rome. Some of their signs read "Iraqi Nazis" and "Iraqi Murderers."

enemies used Soviet-made weapons. It is always necessary to know as much as possible about the enemies' weapons.

Salman told his contact at the embassy in Paris to send an agent to Iraq, call a phone number that he gave them, and ask for someone named Joseph. Meir Amit almost couldn't believe that someone was making this offer. He checked out the story right away. Amit then set up a Mossad agent with a false identity. He would be called George Bacon, and he would travel to Iraq with a false British passport. Iraq was one of Israel's fiercest enemies at the time, and it still is today. It was a dangerous place for an Israeli spy to operate.

"George Bacon" arrived in Baghdad. To shake off suspicion, he acted like an international salesman for a few weeks. Then one day he called Joseph and made an appointment to meet him at a café.

Joseph was a white-haired man who appeared to be in his sixties. He was also Jewish. Jews were a small minority in Iraq. At that time they were not allowed to emigrate from Iraq to Israel. Joseph said he had a nephew who was a pilot in the Iraqi air force. The nephew's name was Munir. Joseph and Munir had come up with a plan to sell a MiG-21 to Israel, then use the money to get the rest of their family secretly out of Iraq.

After meeting Joseph, George Bacon returned to Tel Aviv and told Meir Amit what he had learned. Amit told the amazing story to Prime Minister Ben-Gurion, who approved the complicated covert operation.

Amit put together a complicated plan for stealing the MiG. It involved five separate teams. One group was responsible for conducting radio communication between Baghdad and Israel. Another watched Joseph and Munir's family to make sure they were safe. Yet another team communicated with authorities in Turkey and Washington, D.C. When Munir flew the plane to Israel, it would have to pass over Turkey and American military bases.

Munir had a large family, and he was worried about what would happen to them in Iraq after he stole the MiG. He wanted forty-three of his family members to go to Israel as part of the operation. Amit agreed that Mossad would take care of their safe passage.

First, Mossad deposited half a million dollars into a bank account in Switzerland. A relative of Joseph's traveled to Switzerland to see if the money was there, then called back

Triumphant Israeli soldiers, seen here in June 1967 in the Golan Heights, Syria, return from the Six-Day War. When the fighting ended, Israel had won land four times the size of its original 1948 territory. The Arab population on this land was 1.5 million people.

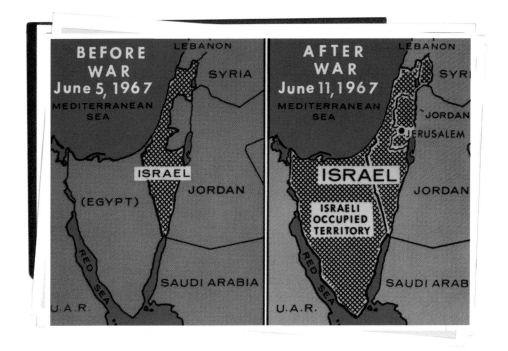

The map on the left shows territories (black and yellow shaded areas) held by Israel on June 5, 1967, before the Six-Day War. The map on the right shows areas held by Israel after the war on June 11, 1967.

to Baghdad and said it was. He did this using a coded message: "The hospital facilities are excellent. I am assured of a total recovery."

Next, Joseph and Munir's family members traveled by car to the mountains near Iraq's border with Turkey. They met a Mossad team that took them to a remote position in the mountains. Turkish helicopters waited there to take them to Israel.

Miraculously, the plan worked. After receiving word that his family was safe, Munir got into the MiG at an airfield in Baghdad. Instead of taking his usual practice run, he flew the MiG across the Turkish border and into Israel.

The stealing of the MiG was a huge show of force by Mossad. It was a difficult, daring international mission and it went off without a problem. Both the Israeli military and the CIA were overjoyed to have such detailed knowledge of the Soviet aircraft. Again Mossad had taken a daring risk and had succeeded.

The Six-Day War

Throughout his time as Mossad chief, Meir Amit continued to run successful intelligence networks. He gathered many Arab informers who gave information for bribes. By 1967, Mossad had agents or informers inside every military base in Egypt. Amit insisted that he needed to know everything. No detail was too insignificant. If an Egyptian officer was an alcoholic, he wanted to know. If the officer was having an affair, he wanted to know that, too. These personal points could be helpful if Mossad needed to blackmail the target. "It was not a pleasant task," said Amit, "but intelligence is often a dirty business."

In May 1967, Amit could see from the information he was getting that Egypt, Syria, and Jordan were planning another attack on Israel in the near future. Instead of waiting for the war, Amit told the Israeli military command that they should assault first, in what is called a pre-emptive strike. On June 5, 1967, Israel attacked. Within six days, Israel took over large parts of Egypt, Jordan, and Syria. Once again, careful intelligence work had paid off.

Meir Amit left his position as director of Mossad in 1968. His ability to expand Mossad's gathering of intelligence, particularly humint, has made him a legend in the world of espionage.

Chapter Six

The New Face of Terrorism

Throughout the 1970s, Israel struggled to combat underground terrorist groups that chose innocent Israeli civilians as their targets. September 5, 1972, was a very sad day in the history of Israel. The Olympics were taking place in Munich, West Germany. A Palestinian terror group called Black September took eleven Israeli athletes hostage. Black September demanded that Israel release 234 prisoners from Israeli jails. Golda Meir, the prime minister of Israel, refused to meet the demands. During an unsuccessful rescue attempt, the terrorists murdered the athletes.

In a private conversation with Mossad director Zvi Zamir, Golda Meir said that Israel would get revenge on the terrorists. Mossad immediately started to carefully track down the people who had participated in the Munich massacre and other crimes. Mossad later carried out the assassination of many of these terrorists. "It was not a simple thing," said Zamir later. "In order to do this, you have to collect information in European states, which is not a legal thing to do."

The assassinations took place outside of Israel, where the terrorists were living under false identities. In Italy, Cyprus, and Greece, individuals connected with Black

In 1972, five Palestinian terrorists entered the Olympic Village in Munich, Germany, taking nine Israeli athletes hostage. They demanded that Israel release more than 200 Arab prisoners. After German police (shown above) attempted a rescue, the hostages were all killed by the terrorists. The terrorists were captured, but they were freed a month later when hijackers of a German jet demanded their release. The terrorists have all since died, most killed by Israeli agents. Abu Daoud, the self-proclaimed mastermind, remains at large.

September, which was a part of the Palestine Liberation Organization (PLO), met their deaths through car bombings, missile attacks on apartments, and other assassination methods. In one case, Mossad officers tracked down Dr. Mahmoud Hamshari, who was the leader of Black September, in France. Mossad felt sure that Hamshari had a role in the Munich massacre. In 1972, he was living in a luxury apartment in Paris. One day, Hamshari was at home when the phone rang. He picked it up and said hello. The voice on the other end said, "Is this Hamshari?" The moment after he replied yes, a powerful bomb exploded in his apartment, killing him. The caller was a Mossad operative.

Spring of Youth

In April 1973, Mossad set up an even more daring operation. The PLO and its leader, Yasser Arafat, were living in Lebanon's capital city, Beirut. Mossad put together a plan called Spring of Youth. The idea was to sneak into Beirut and assassinate senior PLO leaders. On April 10, 1973, a speedboat carrying sixteen Israeli commandos made the seven-hour trip from Israel to Beirut. When they arrived, there were two

The Palestine Liberation Organization (PLO) was established in 1964. In 1969, Yasser Arafat, previously known as Mohammed Abed Ar'ouf Arafat, became its leader. This photo shows Arafat in 1974, at the Arab Summit conference in Rabat, Morocco.

cars waiting for them at the beach. One of the commandos was Ehud Barak, who would later become the prime minister of Israel. The team had decided they would attract less attention if some of them were dressed like women. Mossad agents often pose as couples to divert suspicion. Barak wore a wig and women's clothing, while his Mossad partner posed as the boyfriend.

The couple drove to the home of Kamel Adwan, who was the PLO's chief of operation. When they arrived at the door, they met a guard armed with a rifle. Barak believes that his female disguise created an element of surprise that allowed Mossad agents to shoot the guard before he knew what was

After distinguished careers in the Israeli army and in government, Ehud Barak served as Israel's prime minister and minister of defense from 1999 to 2001. He left office after being defeated by Ariel Sharon.

happening. The Israeli commandos then entered the apartment and assassinated Kamel Adwan. Two other senior PLO officers died that day, and Mossad commandos escaped back to Israel.

Mossad's assassination attempts have not all been successful. On January 7, 1974, Mossad agents in Lillehammer, Norway, killed a Moroccan man named Ahmad Boushiki. They mistakenly thought he was Ali Ahmad Salameh, a PLO leader. Five Mossad agents served prison sentences in Norway as a result of the deadly blunder.

Mossad Today and Tomorrow

While Mossad continues patiently to collect humint and other kinds of intelligence from around the world, there is plenty of information that the organization has not discovered in time.

In 1995, Israel's prime minister Yitzahk Rabin was assassinated by an Israeli man named Yigal Amir. Many people felt that Mossad should have known more about this threat. Shabtai Shavit was Mossad's director general at the time of the Rabin assassination. One Mossad agent has said

Israeli prime minister Yitzhak Rabin, age seventy-three, was assassinated by a Jewish right-wing extremist on November 4, 1995, as he was leaving a mass rally for peace. Rabin had served as Israel's prime minister twice, from 1974 to 1977, and again from 1992 until his 1995 murder. Among the many world leaders who attended his funeral were Egyptian president Hosni Mubarak and American president Bill Clinton, shown above.

that Shavit did warn Rabin that his life may be in danger, but the warning was not specific.

After 9/11

Following the terrorist attacks on the United States on September 11, 2001, the United States has repeatedly stated that Israel is an important ally in the war on terrorism. The CIA and Mossad have been sharing information for many years. It seems likely that Mossad is now helping to investigate the terror network that planned the attacks on the World Trade Center and the Pentagon.

A recent article in the French newspaper *Le Monde* refers to a report that the U.S. Department of Justice

This photograph shows the damage caused on September 11, 2001, when terrorists flew a commercial jetliner into the Pentagon. The impact tore a hole in one side of the heavily reinforced, fifty-five-year-old building and set off a massive explosion and fire. Some experts think that the terrorists meant to hit the White House or Capitol (visible in the background), older buildings that could have been completely destroyed by an airplane attack.

On June 28, 2001, U.S. secretary of state Colin Powell shook hands with Israeli prime minister Ariel Sharon in Sharon's Jerusalem office. Powell had met earlier that day with Palestinian Authority chairman Yasser Arafat. Powell traveled to the Mideast in a bid to save the fragile cease-fire brokered by the United States and signed by Israel and the Palestinians two weeks earlier.

received in June 2001. Compiled by a group of other state agencies including the Drug Enforcement Agency (DEA) and the Federal Bureau of Investigation (FBI), the report claims that in the spring of 2001, 140 Israelis living in the United States were arrested or deported back to Israel. The report states that many of the Israelis were posing as art students, but that they were actually attempting to collect information about U.S. military bases and official buildings.

From December 11 through 14, 2001, the *Carl Cameron Investigates* program on the Fox News Network also reported on this story. Referring to a "vast network" of Israeli spies within the United States, the program also cited sources saying that some of the Israeli agents were

Israeli Defense Forces (IDF) captured a Palestinian Authority-owned freighter, the *Karine A*, in the Red Sea on January 3, 2002. Carrying fifty tons of Iranian-made weapons, the cargo was estimated to be worth more than $100 million. According to Israeli navy admiral Yedidya Ya'ari, the shipment appeared to be headed to terrorists in the West Bank and Gaza Strip. In this photograph, Israeli military chief Lieutenant General Shaul Mofaz (*on the right in the gray shirt*), Prime Minister Ariel Sharon (*center*), and Defense Minister Binyamin Ben-Eliezer (*left*) view the cache.

collecting information about Osama bin Laden's Al Qaeda group, which is believed to be responsible for the September 11 attacks.

Le Monde has reported that five of the Israelis arrested were based in the small town of Hollywood, Florida. Interestingly, four of the five terrorists who hijacked American Airlines Flight 11, which crashed into the World Trade Center, also lived in Hollywood. U.S. and Israeli officials both completely deny all knowledge of these arrests and detentions, dismissing the story as a fantasy. The Fox News Network has since removed the transcript of the show from its Web site.

Other recent events also point to an exchange of information between Mossad and U.S. officials. One example is the case of Iran, which is strategically important to the war on terrorism. On January 4, 2002, Israeli commandos in the Red Sea seized a ship, the *Karine A*, containing a very large shipment of weapons. The *Karine A* had come to the Red Sea from Iran. The arms were headed to the Palestinian territories of Gaza and the West Bank, and it is believed they were to be used in the fight against Israel's occupation of Palestinian lands.

Mossad has stated that the Palestinians have supporters in Iran's Muslim fundamentalist government, and that they had provided the weapons. Secretary of State Colin Powell has also said that he is very concerned about the case of the *Karine A*. Considering that some reports say that Al Qaeda leaders are now hiding in Iran, Israel and the United States may both be worried that people in Iran are arming their enemies.

Ephraim Halevy, Mossad's current director, has made public statements that seem to reveal this concern. During 2002, he pointed out that Iran may pose a nuclear threat to international security. He has also said that moderate, Western-friendly people inside Iran's political structure deserve support from other countries.

Mossad is always ahead of the public in its knowledge of world events. It is impossible to know what Mossad is doing without actually joining the organization, which is very difficult to do. But by studying politics and intelligence trends, it is possible to guess what the agency might be up to. One thing is certain: Mossad will continue to analyze and influence the flow of information around the world. It will continue to use this intelligence to strengthen Israel and the security of its people.

Glossary

agent   A representative or official.

aliyah   Hebrew word for Jews returning to Israel.

ally   Someone who is associated with another as a helper.

assassination   To kill a prominent person by sudden and secret attack.

espionage   The act of spying.

Holocaust   A thorough destruction of a group of people involving extensive loss of life; the mass slaughter of Europeans, especially Jews, by the Nazis during World War II.

humint   Human intelligence.

Jew   A person whose religion is Judaism. A member of a nation existing in the land of Israel from the eleventh century BC to the first century CE.

Palestinian   A person who comes from Palestine, the historic region on the eastern shore of the Mediterranean Sea. Sections of modern Israel, Jordan, and Egypt are all considered to be part of the Palestinian region.

propaganda   Information used to influence someone or something.

sayanim   Jews who help Mossad around the world.

sigint   Signal intelligence.

terrorists People who commit acts of violence, such as bombings, to intimidate a population or government.

Zionist A person who strongly supports Israel's right to exist and defends its security.

For More Information

Anne Frank Center USA, Inc.
584 Broadway, Suite 408
New York, New York 10012
(212) 431-7993

United States Holocaust Memorial Museum
100 Raoul Wallenberg Place SW
Washington, DC 20024-2126
(202) 488-0400

Museum of Jewish Heritage
A Living Memorial to the Holocaust
18 First Place, Battery Park City
New York, NY 10004-1484
(212) 509-6130

Museum of Tolerance
Simon Wiesenthal Plaza
9786 West Pico Boulevard
Los Angeles, CA 90035
(310) 553-8403

Web Sites

Due to the changing nature of Internet links, the Rosen Publishing Group, Inc., has developed an online list of Web sites related to the subject of this book. This site is updated regularly. Please use this link to access the list:

http://www.rosenlinks.com/iwmfia/moss/

For Further Reading

Andryszewski, Tricia. *The Amazing Life of Moe Berg: Catcher, Scholar, Spy.* Brookfield, CT: Millbrook Press, 1996.

Eban, Abba. *My Country: The Story of Modern Israel.* New York: Random House, 1972.

Frank, Anne. *The Diary of Anne Frank.* New York: Bantam Books, 1987.

Lesch, Ann M., and Dan Tschirgi. *Origins and Development of the Arab-Israeli Conflict.* Westport, CT: Greenwood Press, 1998.

Lindwer, Willy. *The Last Seven Months of Anne Frank.* New York: Anchor, 1992

Bibliography

Black, Ian, and Benny Morris. *Israel's Secret Wars: A History of Israel's Intelligence Services.* New York: Grove Weidenfeld, 1991.

CBS News. "An Eye for an Eye." Retrieved November 21, 2001 (http://www.cbsnews.com/stories/2001/11/20/60II/main318655.shtml).

Cypel, Sylvain. "Un réseau d'espionnage israélien a été démantelé aux Etats-Unis." *Le Monde*, May 3, 2002.

Harel, Isser. *The House on Garibaldi Street.* New York: Bantam, 1976.

Pike, John. F.A.S. Intelligence Research Program. Retrieved December 19, 2001 (http://www.fas.org/irp/world/israel/mossad).

Thomas, Gordon. *Gideon's Spies.* New York: St. Martin's Press, 1999.

Westerby, Gerald. *In Hostile Territory: Business Secrets of a Mossad Combatant.* New York: HarperBusiness, 1998.

Index

Credits

About the Author

Matt Webster is a writer living in Brooklyn, New York.

Photo Credits

Cover © Hanan Isachar/Corbis; p. 5 © James A. Sugar/Corbis; pp. 8, 10, 18, 22, 27, 35, 36, 39, 49 © Hulton/Archive/Getty Images, Inc.; pp. 12, 15, 53, 54 © AP/Wide World Photos; pp. 14, 17, 29 © AFP/Corbis; pp. 23, 31, 34, 42, 45, 48 © Bettmann/Corbis; pp. 26, 50 © David Rubinger/Corbis; p. 44 © Victoriano Rastelli/Corbis; p. 51 © Peter Turnley/Corbis; p. 52 © Reuters NewMedia, Inc./Corbis.

Layout and Design

Thomas Forget

Editor

Jill Jarnow